100 Y
Mo
Twen   ictures

100 Years of
Motoring
Twentieth Century in Pictures

AMMONITE
PRESS

PRESS
ASSOCIATION
Images

First Published 2009 by
Ammonite Press
an imprint of AE Publications Ltd,
166 High Street, Lewes, East Sussex BN7 1XU

Text copyright Ammonite Press
Images copyright Press Association Images
Copyright in the work Ammonite Press

ISBN 978-1-906672-33-1

British Cataloguing in Publication Data. A catalogue
record of this book is available from the British Library.

Editor: Daniel Neilson
Series Editor: Paul Richardson
Picture research: Press Association Images
Design: Gravemaker + Scott

Colour reproduction by GMC Reprographics
Printed by Kyodo Nation Printing Services Co., Ltd.

Page 2: A trolleybus, known
as a trackless tram, winds
through London. East Ham
Tramways was one of 50
such systems in the UK
at the beginning of the
20th century.
1912

Page 5: Manufacturers
showcase their latest cars
at the 50th International
Motor Show in London's
Earls Court.
1st October, 1965

Page 6: David Coulthard,
driving a McLaren
Mercedes, takes a turn
along Regent Street as
Formula One comes to
London. Thousands of
F1 fans gathered for the
unprecedented street motor
racing event amid calls for a
permanent Grand Prix to be
staged there.
6th July, 2004

Introduction

Few inventions have impacted human life like the motorcar. When Karl Benz patented his gasoline-engine propelled *Motorwagen* in 1885, it would have been impossible to imagine the vehicle-choked roads we experience today. At the beginning of the 20th century the number of cars in the world was counted in thousands; 100 years later there are more than 600 million. Motoring affects the way we build cities and how we interact socially; it has transformed forever the landscape, the environment, and, following Henry Ford's implementation of the assembly line, the industrial process.

Yet to many, the motorcar is far more than a utilitarian vehicle that exists merely get us from A to B. It is a thing of fascination, pushing the boundaries of science and fulfilling man's seemingly inherent urge to go faster, it is an *objet d'art*; few who look on the E-Type Jaguar or the Aston Martin DB5 would not profess them things of beauty.

Those sleek lines and curves also reflect an age: a photograph can be instantly dated if a car appears in it. During the austere years after the Second World War, the size of cars – and their engines – decreased. Necessity was truly the mother of invention. But the bubble car, once a herald of the future, was soon relegated to the realm of the novelty. More successful was Morris's Mini Minor, probably the most iconic car of the British motoring industry: whether it is John Lennon or Mr Bean behind the wheel the Mini inspires emotion, even if it is one that combines pride with embarrassment.

The remarkable collection of photographs reproduced here, selected from the Press Association's vast archive of more than 15 million images, not only cements Britain's position in the annals of the car and motorcycle industry with names such as Rolls-Royce, Norton and Jaguar, but also in motor racing. The foppish 'Bentley Boys' were racing pioneers as they sped around Brooklands in the supercharged 'Blower' Bentley, leading the way for legends like Stirling Moss, Jim Clark and Lewis Hamilton, while intrepid Britons such as the Campbell dynasty broke dozens of land speed records and continue to do so today.

At every race meet, motor show, car launch or even motorway opening, the Press Association's photographers have captured the daring, the speed, the ingenuity and the humour of those passionate about the motorcar. But far from being a mere pictorial history of the vehicle, this book – whether illustrating grand events or the minutiae of mechanics – is also a history of a nation on the move.

Trams running along the
Victoria Embankment,
London. Electric trams
rumbled through the capital
from 1901 until 1952. In
1999 they began to be seen
in London once again.
1st February, 1904

Facing page: Competitors
in the first South Coast
Motor Rally Championship
in Worthing, Sussex,
waiting expectantly for the
starter's gun.
1st June, 1905

Facing page: Winston Churchill pays off a taxi cab in London when he was President of the Board of Trade and a member of the Liberal Party. The first petrol cabs were introduced in 1903. 'Taximeters' were introduced in 1907, and soon the word 'taxi' became synonymous with 'cab'.
1908

The Honourable Charles Stewart Rolls (R), pioneer motorist and aviator, with a triplane at Shellbeach. Rolls was killed in a plane crash soon after this photograph was taken.
1910

An Automobile Association emergency motorcyclist uses a
new roadside telephone box in Surrey. The AA was formed
on the 29th of June 1905 by a group of motoring enthusiasts,
to help drivers avoid speed traps.
1912

Queen Alexandra watches army
operations from a motor car.
1913

Rush hour at Marble Arch,
London.
1st May, 1913

Protestant Ulstermen, armed with Boer War-era British Army
equipment, pose for the camera. More than 100,000 men
volunteered for the organisation that was set up to resist
Home Rule in Ireland.
1st August, 1913

Motorcycle despatch
riders from the British
Expeditionary Force are
given directions by a French
sentry in northern France
at the beginning of the First
World War.
1st October, 1914

A London horse-drawn cab
pulls up next to its greatest
rival, the car. Equine power
survived in the capital,
however, until 1947.
1st February, 1915

British soldiers of the Royal Artillery hitch a ride on a lorry carrying kit bags to a French port during the First World War.

1916

Women ambulance drivers changing a wheel in 1916.
Between 1914 and 1918 more than 38,000 women worked
as auxiliary nurses, cooks and ambulance drivers in the UK
and on the Western Front.
1916

Women learning to drive trams in London during the First World War.
1918

A rush for trams on the Victoria Embankment in London during a railway strike in 1919. Rail unions had called a nationwide strike over pay.
1919

Violet Cordey before
competing in the Easter
Monday Handicap at
Brooklands racing circuit.
She broke speed records
around the world.
5th April, 1920

Count Zborowski tuning
the 600hp Maybach aero
engine of the car he entered
in Easter Monday racing
heats at Brooklands, the
first dedicated motor racing
circuit in Britain.
14th August, 1920

Count Zborowski's racer, called *Chitty Bang Bang*. The car reached a top speed of 111.92mph. It was to be the first of three cars bearing the name, derived not from the car's noise but from a bawdy soldiers' song that was popular during the Great War.

14th August, 1920

A *K-Type* motor bus, seen in
Westminster.
16th November, 1920

Chitty Bang Bang, next to
the eight horsepower 'GN'
cycle car, affords a striking
contrast during the tuning up
operations at Brooklands.
26th March, 1921

Facing page: Lady
Warrender (R) out for a drive
with friend Audrey James.
14th April, 1921

Count Zborowski in his
Aston Martin, in which he
entered the 1923 French
Grand Prix.
21st October, 1921

HRH Edward, the Prince of Wales, arrives at the Boots factory in Nottingham during a tour of the Midlands.
1st August, 1923

Albert Denly, motorcyclist,
practising at the Brooklands
circuit on his Norton.
6th April, 1925

Welsh driver John Parry
Thomas and Miss Anne
Duke Williams in their high
speed vehicles.
18th April, 1925

Motor racing at Brooklands
in Surrey, the birthplace of
British racing.
2nd May, 1925

King George V and Queen
Mary travelling in an electric
Railodok car at the British
Empire Exhibition, Wembley.
14th May, 1925

Captain Malcolm Campbell
(in plus fours) at the
Skegness Motor Races with
his 350hp V12 *Sunbeam*,
the car with which he broke
the land speed record
at Pendine Sands near
Carmarthen Bay, reaching
146.16mph.
9th June, 1925

Facing page: Tram number
389 to Abbey Wood,
south London, picks up
passengers.
3rd August, 1925

Racing drivers (L-R) Count
Giulio Masetti, Major Henry
Segrave and Count Caberto
Conelli with a Darracq
Special 3 before a 200-mile
race at Brooklands.
25th September, 1925

Facing page: The racers
shoot off the line at the start
of the 200-mile race around
the Brooklands track.
26th September, 1925

A barricaded motor bus passes St Paul's Cathedral during the 1926 General Strike. Called by the Trades Union Congress, the 10 day protest was aimed at improving conditions and pay for coal miners.

7th May, 1926

Facing page: American-born Major Henry Segrave (L), with his mechanic, after winning the 200-mile competition at Brooklands. He went on to break the land speed record in 1929 in his famous *Golden Arrow* car.

26th September, 1925

A food convoy with military
escort during the General
Strike that brought Britain to
standstill.
10th May, 1926

Facing page: Traffic returns to normal across Westminster
Bridge in London following the General Strike. A judgement
found the strike illegal and forced the Trades Union
Congress to abandon the action after 10 days.
18th May, 1926

Aircraftsman T E Shaw on his Brough Superior. Shaw was
better known as T E Lawrence or 'Lawrence of Arabia': First
World War adviser to Prince Faisal during the Versailles Peace
Conference, renowned author and keen archaeologist. He was
killed in a motorcycle accident in 1935.
26th March, 1927

A London County Council
Ambulance.
1929

A Ford van lies crushed after being involved in an accident in London.
1st February, 1929

A greengrocer enjoys a
cigarette as he drives down the
street with his mobile shop.
2nd February, 1929

Jack Dunfee, one of the famous 'Bentley Boys' racing team, fills up at Brooklands petrol station. The group of wealthy motor enthusiasts were known for competing in long distance competitions and won four consecutive chequered flags in the Le Mans 24-hour race between 1927 and 1930.

29th July, 1929

Facing page: Holidaymakers with a new-fangled trailer caravan.

23rd April, 1929

L J Archer edges ahead of
C B Bickell in the Champion
Scratch Race Class at a
British Motorcycle Racing
Club meet at Brooklands.
5th October, 1929

Bentley Boy Clive Dunfee, younger brother of fellow driver Jack, was one of the finest racers of his time. He was killed in an accident during the 1932 500-mile race at Brooklands.

16th October, 1929

A London fireman shows
off a new *Baby Morris* fire
engine.
11th November, 1929

Facing page: Cars, lorries
and buses circle the top of
Aldwych and the Strand in
London.
23rd November, 1929

A motorcyclist with sidecar is soaked during the 'tilting the bucket' competition at a motorcycle gymkhana.
22nd February, 1930

Motor racing through part of the countryside at the Brooklands Racing Circuit.
16th October, 1930

Mobile police with their
motorcycles in London.
21st January, 1931

Facing page: Men work in
the chassis assembly room
of the Morris car factory.
The light *Morris Minor* went
into production in 1928 as a
response to the economic
depression of the time.
21st January, 1931

A London Co-operative
Society milk delivery tanker
makes its rounds in north
London. Daily milk delivery
was essential when few
homes had refrigerators.
4th August, 1931

Facing page: Painting a
white line on the Great West
Road, Osterley, London.
21st October, 1931

Rushing to meet the
deadline: a view of traffic in
Fleet Street, the heart of the
British newspaper industry.
1932

P K Anderson on a Rudge
Whitworth bike at a British
Motorcycle Racing Club
competition at Brooklands.
The manufacturer's motto was
"Rudge it, do not trudge it".
1932

The crushed car of RAF
flying officer George Ivers,
who was killed in a crash in
Bagshot, Surrey.
25th February, 1932

Traffic on Whitechapel Road,
London.
1st April, 1932

Sir Malcolm Campbell's
Bluebird at Brooklands.
Campbell broke five land
speed records in the car,
topping 300mph for the first
time in 1935.
20th April, 1932

A new traffic signalling
device at Ludgate Circus,
London.
19th March, 1932

Racers pose by their cars at Brooklands: (L-R) Brian Lewis,
John Cobb, Tim Rose-Richards and A O Saunder Davis.
20th June, 1932

Karl Sander, stilt walker and former German circus performer, demonstrates a novel way of advertising as he rides alongside a bus in Streatham, south London, on a giant bicycle.

9th August, 1932

Workmen continue to expand
Britain's network of roads.
10th March, 1934

Facing page: Kaye Don powers through Brooklands' puddles.
A month later his accompanying mechanic, Francis Taylor,
was killed during practice on the Isle of Man. Because the
practice session had officially ended, Don was found guilty
of manslaughter and served four months in prison, effectively
ending his career.
28th April, 1934

E Gordon-Simpson and
the young Australian racing
driver, Joan Richmond,
sitting in a 1921 three litre
GP Ballot racer, partaking in
a cigarette before the start of
a race.
7th July, 1934

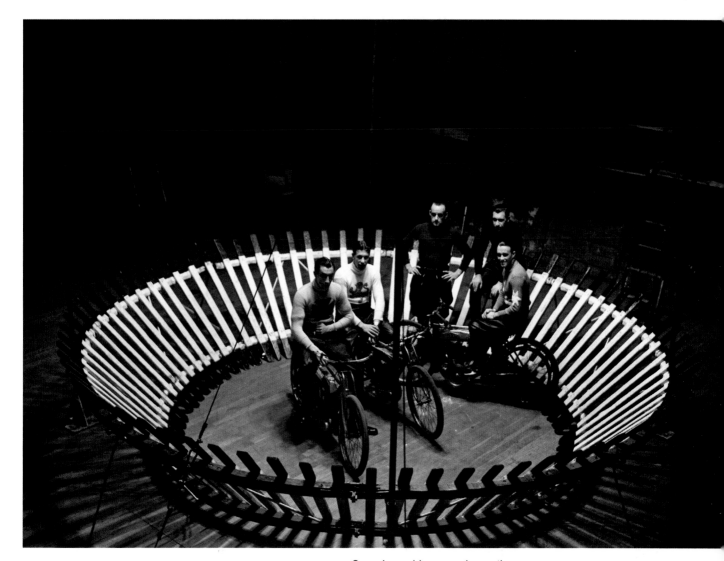

Speedway riders supplementing
their income by riding a circus
'Wall of Death'.
16th October, 1934

A young boy shakes hands
with the driver of a full sized
bus.
15th April, 1935

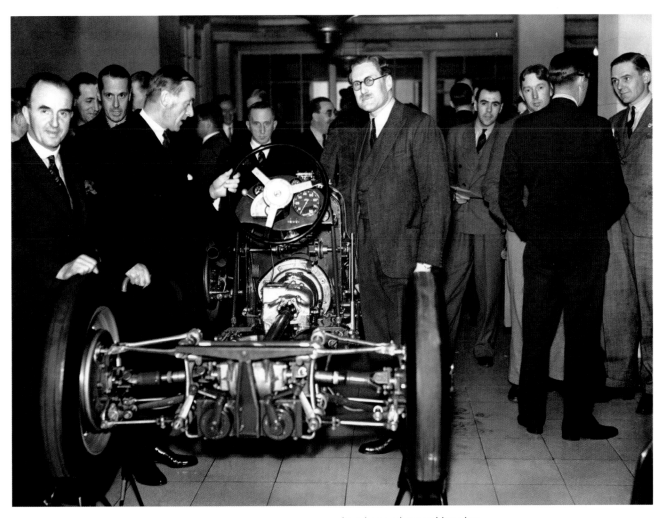

Land speed record breaker,
Malcolm Campbell (second
L), and George Eyston (third
L) with a demonstration
model of an *R-Type* MG.
20th June, 1935

A Carden Lloyd Light Tank, manned by Seaforth Highlanders, blocking a road during army manoeuvres.
7th September, 1935

Motor enthusiasts inspect
the latest models at the
London Motor Show.
23rd September, 1936

Luxury cars being loaded on to the liner *RMS Queen Mary*, destined for the United States.

13th October, 1936

Earl Howe's ERA car being inspected by police after an accident at Brooklands. Howe, who co-founded the British Racing Drivers' Club, later returned to the competition and finished a respectable seventh in the Donington Grand Prix.
1st May, 1937

A congested Piccadilly
Circus before the start of the
Second World War.
1st May, 1939

Miss Patten (Baroness Dorndorf) sits on the door of her Peugeot before the JCC International Trophy at Brooklands.
6th May, 1939

A woman garage attendant
at the beginning of the
Second World War.
12th September, 1939

Facing page: A steel-
helmeted policeman on
duty at the Bank traffic
intersection in London.
2nd September, 1939

Freddy Dixon, known as 'Flying Freddie', mulls over engine parts in his drawing office. He designed a sidecar that leant with the motorcycle.

23rd September, 1939

The racing at Epsom refuses
to stop during wartime, as
seen from this full car park
on Derby Day.
18th June, 1941

Facing page: Princess
Elizabeth receives vehicle
maintenance instruction on
an Austin *10* while serving
with the Mechanised
Transport Training Corps at
Camberley, Surrey.
1945

A fire engine's hose
dampens embers after a
night of heavy bombing in
the capital.
8th September, 1944

War service chiefs in staff cars pass Admiralty Arch during VE day celebrations.
8th August, 1946

Facing page: Traffic chaos in Piccadilly Circus, London.
4th March, 1946

A float carrying the FA Cup,
and members of the winning
Derby County team, rolls
through London during the
Lord Mayor's Show.
9th November, 1946

Admiring crowds watch as
Bob and *Chipona*, trained
to guide blind people,
demonstrate crossing the
road.
14th January, 1947

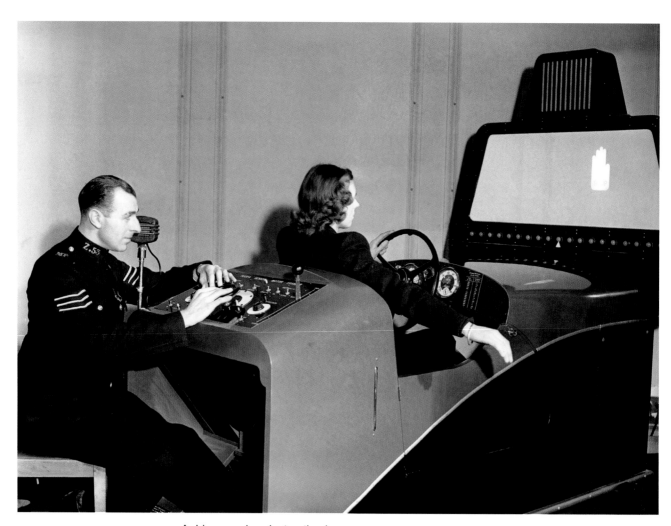

A driver receives instruction in
road safety in a training car.
14th January, 1947

Chelsea's Tommy Walker
(R) points out an interesting
feature in the engine of his
new car to A E Ford (L),
Middlesex Wanderers Rugby
Football Club President.
16th January, 1947

A car churns through
floodwaters in London.
19th March, 1947

Facing page: A police
officer controls the traffic by
loudspeaker and microphone
during the Ascot races.
18th June, 1947

Model racing cars
fascinate a young boy at an
exhibition in the New Royal
Horticulture Hall.
13th August, 1947

A bus tour in London to promote 'Safety First'.
5th September, 1947

Viscount and Viscountess
Curzon beside their Frazer
Nash car at the RAC
Concours D'Elegance in
Regent's Park.
8th September, 1947

Facing page: A Morris
London taxi.
28th November, 1947

Workers putting up signs
in London to direct people
to Wembley Stadium, one
of the venues used during
the 1948 Summer Olympic
Games in London.
1st May, 1948

Top hat and tails are
essential attire no matter
what method of transport
is used to get to Ascot
racecourse.
5th June, 1948

Legendary racing driver
Stirling Moss drives a
Cooper *500* to victory in the
first ever race at Goodwood,
West Sussex.
13th September, 1948

Drivers and mechanics
prepare cars in the pits at
Goodwood.
13th September, 1948

A double-decker bus,
travelling from Worthing to
Brighton, crashed through
a bridge into the Adur river,
trapping 25 people inside.
Fortunately, a low tide meant
all the passengers escaped.
2nd January, 1949

Facing page: Electric signs
light up busy Piccadilly
Circus for the first time since
the Second World War.
4th April, 1949

Motorists on a Surrey road hail an Automobile Association
mobile office. After the Second World War the AA
campaigned to end petrol rationing, which ceased in 1950.
6th April, 1949

Austin Taxis line up along a
London road.
4th May, 1949

Film actress Honor
Blackman, 23, poses on a
Norton motorcycle in Hyde
Park, London.
9th May, 1949

A white-coated policeman
controlling traffic during
a spell of hot weather in
London.
28th June, 1949

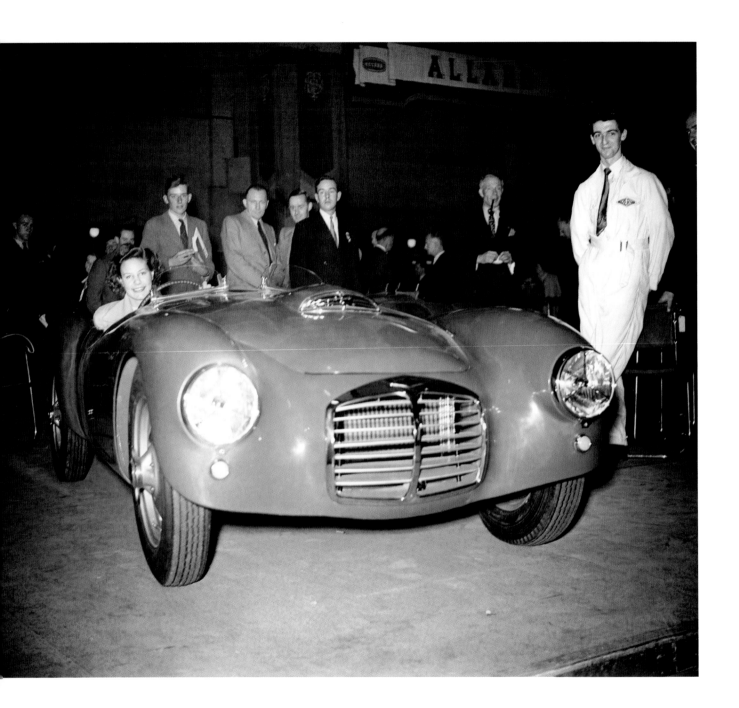

An Alvis *Special* sports
tourer sparkles at the
London Motor Show.
27th September, 1949

Facing page: British
manufacturers Frazer-Nash
show off their new *Mille
Miglia* two litre car at the
London Motor Show at Earls
Court, London.
27th September, 1949

Show jumper Pat Moss,
14 years old, leaps over her
20 year old 'boy wonder'
brother, Stirling, in his racing
car at their father's farm at
Bray, Berkshire.
19th November, 1949

Facing page: Controlling
traffic during a snowstorm in
London.
1950

The glorious interior of a 1950s motorcycle showroom. Machines by BSA, Triumph, Norton, Matchless and others found a ready market before cars were affordable for all. Volume British motorcycle manufacturing effectively ceased in the 1970s, until Triumph re-emerged in 1990. The company now exports worldwide.

1950

London City drivers before embarking on a tour of Europe
with their buses to advertise the 1951 Festival of Britain.
21st June, 1950

Cleaners look at the engine
of a Commer lorry with
interest.
21st September, 1950

Facing page: Morris Minors
line up on the jetty of the
Samuel Williams' Wharf,
London, before being
shipped to Canada after a
million dollar deal.
27th June, 1950

A mobile canteen exhibited
by Jennings and Son during
the Commercial Motor Show
at Earls Court, London.
21st September, 1950

Facing page: An Automobile
Association patrolman digs
out a car that skidded off
an ice-bound road near
Guildford.
15th December, 1950

A 1956 Ford *Zephyr*,
the largest of Ford's UK
passenger cars at the time.
7th April, 1956

A 'Take Your Foot Off'
warning sign that was
erected on the outskirts of
Lancaster in an effort to
persuade motorists to drive
slowly through the town.
1st September, 1956

Triumph's new *TR3*
sports car displayed with
transparent bodywork for the
Motor Show at Earls Court.
16th October, 1956

Facing page: A prototype
Bond *Mark E* minicar. It was
finally launched in 1958, but
teething problems meant
it never caught on and
production stopped after
1,800 were built.
30th October, 1956

A motorist hands over his coupons to a petrol station attendant as fuel rationing begins. Supply shortages were caused when President of Egypt, Gamal Abdul Nasser, took control of the Suez Canal. Panic buying caused havoc around the country.

17th December, 1956

Officers from the Lancashire County Police using the controversial new speed radar gun.
25th July, 1957

A 1907 Hillman stands next
to the manufacturer's latest
model, the 1957 *Minx*.
15th October, 1957

The Austin *A35* gets a
polish during the London
Motor Show at Earls Court,
London.
15th October, 1957

Danish tennis player Kurt
Nielsen getting into a Frisky
microcar at Wimbledon.
These economical vehicles
became popular during the
Suez crisis, which led to
petrol rationing.
23rd June, 1958

Facing page: Two women
deliver sandwiches for the
Motor Scooter Sandwich
Service.
1st July, 1958

Michael Price, Secretary
of Ponsonby Terrace Road
Safety Council, stands with
a placard in protest against
the parking of cars outside
schools in London.
10th July, 1958

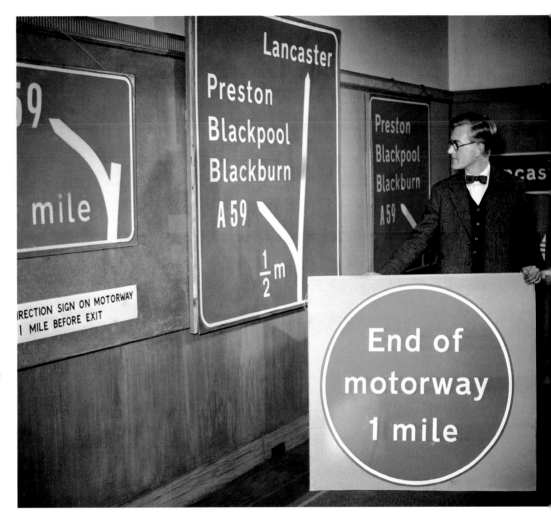

Jock Kinneir with the signs he designed for the Preston bypass motorway. It was the first stretch of motorway in Britain and is now part of the M6. Kinneir, a typographer and graphic designer, with colleague Margaret Calvert, created the model that became the standard for modern road signage in the UK.

1st December, 1958

A vehicle beside one of the signs on the new Preston bypass. Prime Minister Harold Macmillan opened Britain's first motorway on the 5th of December, 1958.

2nd December, 1958

A Jaguar *Mark II* saloon,
which made its debut at the
1959 Paris Motor Show.
1959

A 'Road Flooded' notice
warns motorists that the
River Trent has overflowed
near Twyford, Derbyshire.
23rd January, 1959

A family of four in a Nobel *200*. Britain entered an age of austerity after the fuel shortages of the Suez crisis, and car design reflected this sentiment.
24th February, 1959

Facing page: Carole Carr, a well known stage and TV singer, in her new Sunbeam *Alpine* sports car.
22nd July, 1959

An aerial view of a section of the new London to Birmingham motorway.
7th August, 1959

The new Morris *Mini Minor*
which became one of
Britain's most loved cars.
Designers were told not to
build the car longer than ten
feet.
20th August, 1959

A cut away view of the new
Mini Minor car showing
the front wheel drive
and passenger space.
It was constructed to be
economical.
26th August, 1959

The chassis of a new *Mini Minor* is lowered onto the engine unit. By the time the last *Mini* rolled off the production line in 2000, 5,837,862 cars had been produced.

26th August, 1959

Many stars of the sixties,
including John Lennon,
Marianne Faithfull and Steve
McQueen, owned *Minis*.
28th August, 1959

US President Dwight Eisenhower (standing) waves to the crowds on Fleet Street as he is driven to St Paul's Cathedral with British Prime Minister Harold Macmillan (seated in back seat).

31st August, 1959

The Lotus *Seven* car could be supplied as a kit to avoid
Purchase Tax. The tax loophole could be exploited only
if no assembly manual was included, so Lotus offered
'disassembly' instructions, telling owners to follow them
backwards.
2nd September, 1959

Traffic is seen streaming on
and off the Chiswick Flyover,
the last section of a £6m road
scheme in London. Actress
Jayne Mansfield added some
glamour to the project when
she cut the ribbon.
30th September, 1959

Facing page: A glittering
assembly of the latest cars
ready for the opening of
the London Motor Show at
Earls Court.
20th October, 1959

The first cars speed along
Britain's first full-length
motorway, the M1 between
London and Leeds.
2nd November, 1959

An Automobile Association
road service van tows a
broken down car.
2nd November, 1959

A motorist uses an
emergency telephone on the
new London to Birmingham
M1 motorway.
2nd November, 1959

Air Vice-Marshall Donald
Bennett (L) and W Banks
wait to check in their
Fairthorpe car at the RAC
British International Rally at
Crystal Palace, London.
20th November, 1959

Racing sensation Stirling
Moss rockets around Brands
Hatch in a Porsche.
25th August, 1960

Facing page: Engineer Leo
Villa (L) talks to Donald
Campbell, son of Malcolm
Campbell, who is seated
at the wheel of his turbine
powered *Bluebird* car.
18th July, 1960

The new *MGA*. It had a top
speed of 96mph and could
accelerate from 0 to 60mph
in 13.3 seconds.
27th September, 1960

The Morris *Mini Minor*, cut
away for closer inspection,
at the 1960 London Motor
Show.
18th October, 1960

The new *Travelette*
caravan in closed position.
Caravanning holidays
became extremely popular
throughout the 1960s.
22nd March, 1961

Mike Hailwood, considered to be one of the greatest British motorcycle racers of all time, bolts around Brands Hatch. He went on to win the gruelling Isle of Man TT 12 times.

29th April, 1961

Taking notes at a 1961 traffic census checkpoint in Dalton, Yorkshire.
11th September, 1961

Adding some glamour to the London Motor Show at Earls Court, bikini-clad model Eve Eden, 21, poses on the bonnet of a Sunbeam *Alpine*.

17th October, 1961

The 4.5 litre V8 Daimler
Limousine at the 1961
London Motor Show.
18th October, 1961

The *Hover Rover*, an air
cushioned long wheelbase
Land Rover, is tested at a
military vehicle exhibition.
Weight proved a problem for
the vehicle and it was never
put into production.
27th September, 1962

Three young models show
off the space inside a new
Hillman at the London Motor
Show.
16th October, 1962

Karen Birch lifts a Peel *P50*, the world's smallest car. It weighs a mere 132lb (59kg).
8th November, 1962

Facing page: One of London's latest double-decker *Routemaster* buses is swung aboard the Cunard cargo liner *Alaunia* at King George V Dock, London. The bus was en route to Philadelphia, where it featured in the Exposition Britannia.

12th September, 1963

Paddy Hopkirk (L) and his co-driver Henry Liddon with the *Mini Cooper S*, the car they drove to victory in the 1964 Monte Carlo Rally.

27th January, 1964

The Beatles in a chauffeur driven vintage Rolls-Royce at ABC Television studios at Teddington, where the group was taking part in recording sessions.
23rd February, 1964

Facing page: A driver approaches the prototype of an illuminated hazard warning sign for motorways at Hendon, London.
5th February, 1964

Mods Roy Young and Linda
Jarvis on Derby Sunday on
the Epsom Downs, with their
fully-dressed scooter.
31st May, 1964

Extra police were required at Hastings after outbreaks of trouble between scooter riding Mods and motorcycling Rockers who descended on the Sussex resort.

2nd August, 1964

Jim Clark, one of motorsport's greatest drivers, sits in his Lotus 30 Ford car before a race at Goodwood. He won the 1963 and 1965 Formula One World Championships, but his career was cut tragically short by a fatal crash in a 1968 Formula Two race.

28th August, 1964

The new Austin *1800* five seater.
13th October, 1964

Facing page: Actress Laya
Raki and the Aston Martin
DB5 were eye catchers at
the London Motor Show at
Earls Court.
20th October, 1964

Clouds of spray, indicative of the dicey conditions on the
Silverstone track, are thrown up behind the duelling John
Surtees in a Lola *Traco* (R) and Jim Clark in a Lotus Ford.
Although Surtees spun six times in the last eight laps he was
still classified second behind winner Clark.
20th March 1965

The cast of the new edgy
police series *Z-Cars*.
27th September, 1965

Long, low and sleek lines
of the Jaguar *E-Type*
sports car.
1st October, 1965

A new 70mph speed limit sign. An increase in accidents led to the introduction of a national speed limit.
7th December, 1965

Transport Minister Tom Fraser (L) demonstrating the breathalyser
to Home Secretary Sir Frank Soskice. Secret documents
released in 1995 revealed Harold Wilson's government's concern
that its introduction would turn voters away.
21st December, 1965

The Jaguar 4.2 litre *E-Type*.
In 2008 the *Daily Telegraph*
crowned the iconic British
sports car as the most
beautiful car of all time.
7th March, 1966

The Peel *Trident* four-wheel
baby car that weighs
only 198lb.
21st March, 1966

Mrs Carmelita Roach, is one of the first two black people to become traffic wardens in Britain.
16th April, 1966

A revolutionary battery powered
chariot, designed for whisking
busy executives around the
factory floor, is demonstrated
at the Mechanical Handling
Exhibition at Earls Court,
London.
9th May, 1956

Comedian and motor
enthusiast Peter Sellers
photographs the Unipower
GT Mini.
10th May, 1966

A Ford *Popular* was given a brickwork paint job for Mrs Rennie Hughes of Leeds.
4th October, 1966

German actress Margit Saad (R) and Jean Herbert-Smith
towing the lightweight Sprite *400* caravan around Bryanston
Square in London.
4th December, 1966

The start of the tobacco-sponsored WD & HO Wills Trophy at Silverstone.
27th March, 1967

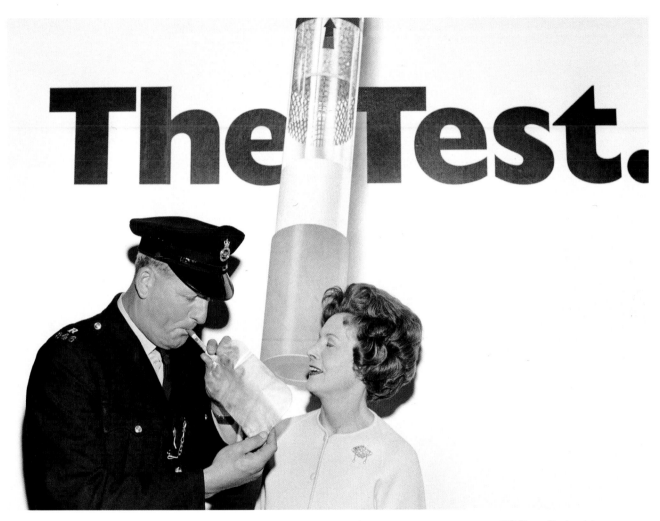

The Test.

Facing page: New Zealand-born Denny Hulme in a Ford *GT 40* at Silverstone. Hulme became the 1967 Formula One World Champion.
27th March, 1967

PC Tony Burton blows into the *Alcotest 80* for the Transport Secretary Barbara Castle, as she launches a campaign informing the public of the new breathalyser law.
27th March, 1967

Facing page: A bus-only lane over Vauxhall Bridge, London. It was the first day of an experiment to give buses a lane of their own during evening rush hours.
26th February, 1968

Cars drive off the first cross-channel hovercraft service at Dover. The Mountbatten Class craft, the largest in the world, can transport 30 cars and 254 passengers to Boulogne.
30th July, 1968

A Ford *Doppelganger* built
specifically for the Gerry
Anderson film of the same
name. The £10,000 car is
capable of speeds up to
140mph.
9th October, 1968

Motorcycle police escort
American President Richard
Nixon from Claridge's Hotel
to Number 10 Downing
Street for talks with Prime
Minister Harold Wilson.
25th February, 1969

A Lotus Ford car in action at
Brands Hatch.
14th March, 1969

Prince of Wales steps out of
his blue *MGC* after driving
to the University College of
Wales to begin a course.
21st April, 1969

Racing driver Jackie Stewart, nicknamed the 'Flying Scot', is joined by a model to advertise Dunlop tyres. Stewart won three Formula One World Driver's Championships between 1965 and 1973.
1st July, 1969

Vicky Ward and Cynthia
Cassidy on a Raleigh
Supermatic moped.
9th November, 1969

Manchester United and Northern Ireland footballer George Best stands by his Manchester Boutique and MG.

6th January, 1970

Traffic flows in both directions for the first time on the new London Bridge.
23rd February, 1970

West Ham United footballer
Jimmy Greaves swaps a
football for a steering wheel.
5th March, 1970

Tony Jacklin, first British winner of the US Open golf championship for 50 years, rides in a vintage white Cadillac at the head of a motorcade in his home town of Scunthorpe, Lincolnshire.
24th June, 1970

Julie Ege, a former Miss
Norway, graces the bonnet
of a Ford *Cortina 2000*.
13th October, 1970

Facing page: A policeman is silhouetted by car headlamps
trying to sort out rush hour chaos in Bristol. The thickest fog
for many years, combined with the voluntary switching off of
street lighting to relieve an electricity shortage, caused huge
traffic jams.
14th December, 1970

Despite the nationwide postal strike, Mrs Fay Taylor continues her round on a motorcycle.

25th January, 1971

An understandably cheerful
Prince of Wales at the wheel
of his Aston Martin *DB6*
sports car.
4th February, 1971

A model gives away free
ice cream while sitting on
the bonnet of a Lamborghini
Espada on the forecourt of a
Shell garage in London.
1st May, 1971

The final section of the
M4 after being opened by
Michael Heseltine, junior
minister at the Department of
Transport.
22nd December, 1971

Harry and Frances Gilbert from West Twyford with their nine year old son Kristy, have spent five days of their holiday in their parked caravan. They were due to spend their break in Bournemouth but the clutch on their Rover burned out on the Kingston bypass.
3rd April, 1972

Facing page: Britain's most famous motorway intersection, known as 'Spaghetti Junction', opens in Birmingham.
18th May, 1972

Motorcycles of fans
attending the Rock 'n' Roll
Revival Festival at Wembley
Stadium.
5th August, 1972

British racing driver Jackie
Stewart (R) with Brazilian
Emerson Fittipaldi and their
Ford *Capri RS 2600* before a
race in Germany.
5th July, 1973

Facing page: Lyn Worral,
21, is an optional extra with
this Meccano beach buggy,
pictured at the Waldorf
Hotel, London.
22nd November, 1973

A mounting crisis grips Britain as motorists continue their
hunt for ever-dwindling petrol supplies. The shortage was
caused when the Organisation of Arab Petroleum Exporting
Countries held back supply to increase prices.
4th December, 1973

Farmer Cyril Bray decides
on true horsepower as the
petrol shortage worsens.
6th December, 1973

Model Sue Longhurst
stands in front of a hand-
built Jensen *Interceptor*
convertible at the London
Motor Show at Earls Court.
15th October, 1974

Testing out a two-seater
electric vehicle at Bawtrey,
near Doncaster.
12th February, 1975

American stunt rider Evel Knievel attempting a leap over 13 buses at Wembley Stadium. He was severely injured and hospitalised when he crashed.

26th May, 1975

An Austin *Allegro 1500 Super Estate*. Despite being referred to as the 'All-Aggro' by drivers bemoaning its unreliability, it was a very popular car and remained in production until 1983.
4th June, 1975

Motorcycles ready for delivery at the Small Heath plant of Norton-Villiers-Triumph. Norton-Villiers Ltd – one of NVT's nine subsidiaries – went into liquidation following the government's decision not to pump any more money into the motorcycle group.

1st August, 1975

The stylish two-seater
Triumph *TR7* is launched
by Leyland Cars. The car
clocked up £24m in sales
thanks to its superior
performance and comfort.
19th May, 1976

Facing page: An example of the 25 silver buses
commissioned to operate on several busy routes as a
London Transport contribution to celebrations marking the
Queen's Silver Jubilee.
6th July, 1976

James Hunt celebrates as he takes the chequered flag to win the British Grand Prix at Brands Hatch. He was disqualified two months later for illegally using a spare car after a pile-up on the first lap forced the race to be restarted.
18th July, 1976

Facing page: The stars of *The New Avengers*: (L-R) Gareth Hunt as *Gambit*, Joanna Lumley as *Purdey* and Patrick MacNee as *Steed*, stand by their equally stylish cars: a Jaguar *XJS*, an *MGB Roadster* and a rather vulgar Jaguar *XJ6*!
12th October, 1976

The Marquess and
Marchioness of Tavistock
with their son Jamie and
a £32,000 Aston Martin
Lagonda outside their home,
Woburn Abbey.
24th April, 1978

Facing page: Queen Elizabeth II and the Duke of Edinburgh are
driven around Sydney Cricket Ground before a Rugby League
match during the Silver Jubilee year. Protesters in the crowd
display a placard that reads 'Republic for Australia'.
13th March, 1977

PC Alec McHattie testing
a new hand-held speed
detection device.
1st December, 1978

Upended cars after gale-
driven seas swept over
Chesil Beach, Dorset.
13th February, 1979

The Humber Bridge, briefly
the world's longest single
span suspension bridge,
during construction.
21st March, 1980

Jake Mangel Wurzel and his extraordinary *Wurzel-Wagon*.
The former lorry driver, born John Grey, changed his name
by deed poll when he appointed himself Huddersfield's
unpaid entertainer.
1st May, 1980

The first British Leyland-produced *Mini Metros* on the assembly line at the multi-million pound plant at Longbridge, Birmingham.
8th October, 1980

Lady Diana Spencer leaving
her Earls Court flat with a
new *Mini Metro,* en route to
her job as a kindergarten
teacher.
17th November, 1980

One of 12 specially
decorated buses that London
Transport operated to
commemorate the wedding
of Charles and Diana.
9th January, 1981

Motorcycle stuntman
Eddie Kidd jumps over five
spectators' cars.
19th May, 1981

Facing page: The Prince and Princess of Wales drive through Romsey on their way to Broadlands, the home of Lord Mountbatten, for their honeymoon.
29th July, 1981

Destroyed cars in the aftermath of a night of violent rioting in the Toxteth district of Liverpool.
5th July, 1981

A sympathetic building
society manager organises
a 'house' for a couple who
have been gazumped five
times.
21st August, 1981

The Northern Irish-made DeLorean sports car. It became
famous for being turned into a time machine for the film *Back
to the Future*, which saved it from being remembered only as
a spectacular failure of the development grant concept.
5th October, 1981

Model *Tula* poses alluringly at the Supernation Custom Car Show at Olympia in London. Former Bond girl *Tula* was later famously 'outed' as a transsexual by the tabloid press.

30th October, 1981

Stockpiled DeLorean cars waiting to be exported from the plant in Belfast to the United States.

1st February, 1982

Former Formula One World
Champion Jackie Stewart
poses next to a new Ford
Orion.
4th May, 1982

London businessman
Richard Noble with the
turbojet *Thrust II*, the car in
which he later broke the land
speed record at 633mph.
23rd May, 1983

A double-decker bus points
to the sky after reversing into
a large hole in the road.
12th October, 1983

Members of the *Hell's Angels* motorcycle group outside a £100,000 farmhouse on the Woburn Abbey estate where they lived rent-free. There were rumours that the estate's owner, Lord Tavistock, may have given in to threats.
14th May, 1984

Inventor Mike Barnes rides
around Parliament Square
on the *Nippi* motorbike,
designed to take both rider
and wheelchair.
17th July, 1984

The scene on the north side of the Humber Bridge as angry motorists find their way blocked by the cars of picketing miners. The coal miners were protesting against the closure of 'unprofitable' mines.

24th July, 1984

Trade and Industry Secretary
Norman Tebbit in a Leyland
Roadrunner on the day it
was launched.
25th September, 1984

Inventor Sir Clive Sinclair demonstrating his famous flop, the *C5* electric vehicle.
10th January, 1985

One of Britain's most successful Grand Prix motorcycle racers,
the charismatic Barry Sheene, with his wife Stephanie.
1st July, 1985

Formula One star Nigel Mansell in discussion with his pit
crew as engineers work on his car during practice day for the
British Grand Prix at Brands Hatch. Mansell won the race,
his first Formula One victory.
11th July, 1986

Facing page: A rain-drenched Birmingham is turned into a racing track for the Super Prix, a motor racing meeting held on a street circuit at the heart of the city from 1986 to 1990. The main event was a round of the European Formula 3000 Championship, with support races including BTCC and Formula Ford 1600 rounds, as well as sports car racing. Laid out on public roads the circuit was notoriously bumpy.

25th August, 1986

"*You can't park there, mate*": a *Mini* balances on its big brother, a *Maxi*, after crashing from the top storey of a car park.

4th September, 1986

A new *Metrocab* taxi picks up a fare on London's Westminster Bridge. The five passenger city cab can accommodate disabled passengers.
10th December, 1986

Prime Minister Margaret
Thatcher tries out a new
breathalyser at a factory in
Barry, South Glamorgan.
26th May, 1987

Project manager Richard
McKechnie promotes
GE Vector's prototype
plastic car.
13th May, 1988

Fans of British racing driver Nigel Mansell display a
banner at Silverstone during the 1988 British Grand Prix.
They left disappointed as Brazilian Ayrton Senna took the
chequered flag.
10th July, 1988

Film star Bob Hoskins (R) and Lord Winchilsea, founder
of the Saharaman Aid Trust, outside the House of Lords,
before setting off on a charity drive to Southern Algeria.
More than 15 Land Rovers and a London taxi raised money
for Saharawi refugees living in camps since their land was
annexed by Morocco 13 years previously.
19th February, 1989

A motorist fills up at Rossmore Court petrol station, London, which claimed to be Europe's first completely unleaded petrol station.

14th March, 1989

The bespoke 1970 Mercedes
Benz *600 Pullman* limousine,
originally owned by John
Lennon, before it was
auctioned.
27th April, 1989

Facing page: Prime Minister
Margaret Thatcher (R)
and Lady Porter, leader of
Westminster City Council,
driving a high-pressure water
street cleaning machine
outside 10 Downing Street.
It was part of a Westminster
initiative for clean streets.
14th April, 1989

The Lotus *Elan* convertible.
It had a top speed of 137mph
and could accelerate from 0
to 60mph in 6.5 seconds.
17th October, 1989

A Rolls-Royce in production at its factory in Crewe. In 1990, German manufacturers BMW bought Vickers, the parent company of Rolls-Royce.
26th April, 1990

Facing page: The new Jaguar *XJ200*, the fastest production car in the world with a top speed of 223mph, is given its first public outing on Austria's Salzburgring circuit.
13th August, 1992

Robots at work on the Rover *200 Series* at the increasingly mechanised production line at Longbridge car plant in Birmingham.
15th July, 1992

The new retro-styled Rover
MG RV8 sitting next to a
1962 *MGB*.
12th October, 1992

Colin McRae (R) and his co-driver Derek Ringer celebrate their World Rally Championship victory at Chester Race Course.
22nd November, 1995

Minis were not designed for these conditions: a stranded driver checks on the condition of her car trapped in a snowdrift near Dover, Kent.
21st February, 1996

A Vauxhall *MAXX*, the company's concept car, drives past Buckingham Palace. The vehicle is capable of returning 72mpg.

6th May, 1996

In celebration of the centenary of the British motor industry, a Jaguar *XJ220* is covered in silver sedum for the Chelsea Flower Show.
15th May, 1996

Facing page: Methley Terrace, Leeds, is covered in turf to launch Transport 2000's 'Streets For People' campaign, designed to encourage people to reduce the amount of traffic in their neighbourhoods.
16th August, 1996

The TVR Cerbera supercar
is unveiled at Birmingham's
NEC during the British
International Motor Show.
The seven litre car has a top
speed of 240mph.
15th October, 1996

Environmental campaigner Daniel Hooper, known as Swampy, spent a week in a complex series of tunnels dug in the path of an extension to the A30 road in Fairmile, Devon, resisting eviction by police, and later participated in a tunnel protest against the building of a second runway at Manchester Airport.
31st March, 1997

The scourge of motorists everywhere, private wheel clampers in central London pounce on PA photographer Adam Butler's car after he was targeted as being illegally parked – after only one minute.
31st December, 1997

Facing page: Don Wales, nephew of Donald Campbell and grandson of Sir Malcolm Campbell, unveils the *Bluebird* electric car in which he continued his family tradition of setting world land speed records. Mr Wales smashed the British electric speed record by reaching 146mph.
24th September, 1997

Barrister Michael Shrimpton,
head of the newly formed
Rolls-Royce Action
Committee, announces a
bid to buy out the luxury car
makers.
8th January, 1998

The latest handmade *Blenheim 2*, built by the luxury vehicle company Bristol Cars, goes on sale for £118,778. Only 100 were made and celebrity fans, including Oasis rock star Liam Gallagher and Virgin boss Richard Branson, snapped them up.
14th January, 1998

Co-driver Adrian Biles checks the route as he sits in his 1950
Jaguar *XK120* at Brooklands in Surrey. One hundred and
eighty classic car enthusiasts gathered at Britain's first motor
racing circuit for the Monte-Carlo Challenge 1998 – the
largest classic car rally in Europe.

8th February, 1998

Car connoisseurs peer into
a pristine Jensen *Interceptor
Mark III*.
7th June, 1998

Mechanic Trevor Hatton
relaxes in his *Mini*-themed
house in Cheltenham.
7th August, 1998

Richard Brown attempts
the British land speed
record in his rocket powered
motorcycle at Elvington
Airfield near York. The
record attempt was beset
with problems including poor
weather, stray animals and
a broken speedometer, but
still achieved a phenomenal
365mph.
14th October, 1998

Heavy traffic near Heathrow on the M25. The motorway has
been described as the world's largest car park.
23rd October, 1998

Deputy Prime Minister John Prescott during a photocall at London's King's Cross Station to launch a new Motorail service between London and Aberdeen.

29th March, 1999

Facing page: A sculpture
made of cars the DVLA have
scrapped for not having a
tax disc.
20th April, 1999

Trade and Industry Secretary Stephen Byers (L) with BMW
chairman Professor Joachim Milberg outside the Department
of Trade and Industry in London, with a new Rover 75.
German car giant BMW was to invest more than £3bn in
Britain over the following six years, but by 2008 no Rover
cars were being built.
23rd June, 1999

Travellers (and animals)
make their way around the
Lizard Peninsula of Cornwall,
as thousands flock to the
south west the day before a
total solar eclipse.
9th August, 1999

The super lightweight
Lotus *Elise 340R* at The
Hippodrome in London's
Leicester Square, before
going on sale for £35,000.
12th August, 1999

Andy Shacklock puts the solar-powered car, *Mad Dog III*, through its paces before heading to Australia to compete in the 2,000 mile World Solar Challenge. It has a top speed of 58mph – on a sunny day.

26th August, 1999

A McLaren *F1*, the fastest
production car ever built,
reached speeds of 240mph.
Only 106 were ever made.
16th January, 2000

Workers cheering as the 5,387,862nd and final classic *Mini* rolls off the production line of the MG Rover Group factory at Longbridge, Birmingham. After 41 years of continuous production and nearly 140 different models, one of Britain's best loved cars was superseded by a redesigned version from German car giant BMW.

4th October, 2000

The *XK8* 'Shaguar' Jaguar, which was used in *Austin Powers: International Man of Mystery*, a spoof film about a 1960s secret agent.
17th June, 2002

Workers wave goodbye to the last ever Rolls-Royce to be built at the luxury car maker's plant at Crewe. After 56 years, production moved to Goodwood, West Sussex, under BMW's management.
30th August, 2002

Bentley's *Continental GT Coupe* has a final polish before making its UK debut at the British International Motor Show at the NEC in Birmingham.
22nd October, 2002

TV's *Top Gear* presenter
Jeremy Clarkson leans on
a two seater, tilting three
wheeled *Carver*, which has
the comfort, controls and
stability of a normal car
with the dynamic cornering
behaviour of a motorcycle.
4th September, 2003

Workers inspect a Jaguar *XK*
as it rolls off the production
line at the company's
Castle Bromwich plant in
Birmingham.
20th December, 2005

Conservative Party leader David Cameron with a Reva *G-Wiz*, a carbon neutral electric car, as he committed the Conservatives to slashing carbon emissions on British roads.
24th April, 2006

A vandalised speed camera
sign on London Road.
14th November, 2006

An original *Batmobile* from the 1960s television series *Batman* outside New Scotland Yard in central London.
18th February, 2007

Facing page: Headlights and taillights trace the passage of traffic on the M3 motorway at dusk.
18th January, 2007

A tipper truck wedged
underneath a motorway sign
after a freak accident on the
M80.
22nd February, 2007

The Prince of Wales with
a new eco-friendly Honda
Civic car during a test drive
around the car park of the
Hampton Court Palace.
4th June, 2007

Dreams of freedom: a
camper van on the beach
at Weston-Super-Mare,
Somerset.
18th June, 2007

A vehicle decorated with
traffic cones at the 2007
Glastonbury Festival.
22nd June, 2007

A car abandoned in the
snow on the A68 near
Castleside, County Durham.
1st February, 2008

Facing page: New *Minis*
lined up on Southampton
Docks waiting to be
exported.
7th December, 2007

'Juice points', for the charging of electric cars, are introduced on the streets of London. They are located next to specially designated free parking spots around the capital.

8th May, 2008

Test driver Don Wales, grandson of Sir Malcolm Campbell, walks towards his British-built steam car before attempting to break the land speed record for a steam powered vehicle.
25th June, 2005

McLaren Mercedes' Lewis Hamilton celebrates winning the British Grand Prix at Silverstone. On the 2nd of November 2008, 23 year old Hamilton became the youngest ever Formula One World Champion after a dramatic race at the Brazilian Grand Prix.

6th July, 2008

Participants cross Westminster Bridge past the Houses of Parliament during the 2008 London to Brighton Veteran Car Run.
2nd November, 2008

The Publishers gratefully acknowledge Press Association Images, from whose extensive archive the photographs in this book have been selected. Personal copies of the photographs in this book, and many others, may be ordered online at www.prints.paphotos.com

PRESS
ASSOCIATION
Images

For more information, please contact:

Ammonite Press

AE Publications Ltd. 166 High Street, Lewes, East Sussex, BN7 1XU, United Kingdom
Tel: 01273 488005 Fax: 01273 402866
www.ammonitepress.com